How to **HELP**
Your Student
SUCCEED in School

A Guide For Parents and Students

Paul Kip Grimm

ISBN: 1453708197
ISBN-13: 9781453708194
Library of Congress Control Number: 2010910621

"My dear friend Kip Grimm was destined to teach ! I earnestly recommend" How to Help Your Student Succeed In School, A Guide For Parent's and Students "as a must read for both parents and students who want to acquire the principles and answers to succeeding in the academic arena."

Barbara Lazaroff, Mother, restaurateur, designer, co-author of *"Wishes for a Mother's Heart"*, philanthropist

"This experienced educator and parent shares foolproof tools and specific steps to insure student success in school. Practical and easy to follow, this book is just the roadmap you need to make serious, positive change that leads to joyful learning for even the most struggling of students. Written with expertise, understanding, and compassion, How to Help Your Student Succeed in School is a game changer."

**Susan A. Nelson Head of Schools
The Webb Schools of California**

"Mr. Grimm gives you a proven hands-on blueprint for the academic (and life) success of your child. Your child will be forever grateful ."

Larry T. Earley, Marriage and Family Life Coach

"Kip Grimm presents a work unique in its ability to reach students and parents precisely on a level at which they can relate, question, and respond. It is well worth reading and following"

Dr. Charlene Moskovitz Zimbroff M.D. Psychiatrist

"How To Help Your Student Succeed In School, A Guide For Parent's and Student's presents an easily understood guide to setting the stage for educational success and life long learning"

Dr. Marilyn E. Shipley Ed.D. Coordinator of Curriculum, Riverside County Superintendent of Schools

Dedication

This book is dedicated to all
students, parents,
grandparents, and guardians
who want to make a difference.

MISSION

to provide parents and students with tools to promote immediate success in their educational process

I believe every student can be 100% more successful in school.

All they need are the skills to start their foundation of learning.

Once they establish good habits of learning, their entire life (and yours) will improve.

The earlier you start, the easier it will become.

PREFACE

There has never been a time when our education system was so stressed as it is now.

Bigger classes and fewer days are becoming more and more common.

This book is written for all parents and students who want a head start to being successful in any class. If you follow these simple steps, I guarantee you will raise your grade and be in the good graces of every teacher!

With education in crisis, we must take action to see that our children receive the maximum from their school experience. Not only does school provide social networking skills for students, it provides a way students can help themselves take *full advantage* of their education possibilities.

FORWARD

I had been teaching 20 years when I unexpectedly

had my nephew come live with me. It was the end of his sixth grade and he was flunking out. He had to attend double summer school just to get into the seventh grade.

Being a teacher, I thought it would be easy to help him get through his school years. When the first progress report arrived, I was shocked to see such bleak remarks. "Homework not in, not participating in class, polite but always looks tired." I realized I had to take an active part in his education.

I got to know every teacher of every subject he took that year, and visited them on a weekly basis. What I learned was that it took my constant involvement with his school and teachers for him to be successful.

In my nephew's sophomore year of high school, he took a chemistry class that was very difficult for him. I didn't know much about chemistry and was not much help to him. He ended up failing the class and had to take it again in summer school. I already had my summer planned, and I was surely not happy that not only did he fail the class but I was going to have to change my summer plans to accommodate taking him to school early every morning and picking him up on my lunch hour.

I decided it was time for a serious talk. We had a conversation and I discussed with him my expectations of him for the summer.

The first day after class, I went in and introduced myself to the teacher, let her know I wanted my nephew to succeed in the class, and asked for her input. My nephew was with me for the meeting.

From then on I made it my business to arrive early about three times a week when class was out and just say hi and ask for a verbal report of my nephew's progress.

When he came home from school, all his studying and homework had to be done before any electronics could be turned on. No music, television, or computer. When I came home in the evening, the first thing I did was check his homework. He knew I was serious about this. He also had to change his bedtime to allow for eight hours of sleep every school night. In the morning he was to shower, have breakfast, and be waiting at the door with his homework when it was time to leave.

He was not to have me wait one minute. (Of course, this meant that I had to be on time also.)

At first he balked, but as the days passed he seemed to get happier and started liking the class more and more. I attribute this change to his being ready for class, arriving on time with his homework done, and being prepared by actually reading the assigned pages.

It also didn't hurt that he was getting enough sleep every night and having breakfast in the morning.

He got to know the teacher, and he and I both developed a rapport with her. She was a fantastic, caring teacher.

When the last day of class arrived, he was excited to take the final exam.

We were surprised and thrilled later that evening when he got a personal call from the teacher saying how proud she was of him. Not only did he get an A on the final, he earned an A in the class! She knew he would be happy with the results of his efforts, and proud to tell me of his success.

My lesson in all this was seeing things from the other side of the desk—the parent's side!

I encourage all parents, guardians, grandparents, aunts and uncles, sisters, brothers, and caretakers of students not to wait another day. Get involved in all aspects of your student's education.

There is no greater Blessing.

Table of Contents

FOR STUDENTS   83

GOALS

My goal as an educator and your goal as a concerned parent in regards to your student's education are the same.

We want our student to be excited about education, eager to learn, graduate with a goal for the future, and have a plan on how to get there!

Along the way, we want students to discover what interests them and then work towards a career in that field using critical thinking skills to solve problems, as well as to be able to research any information they are looking for.

Anyone can look up information online or in a book, but critical thinking goes beyond that and involves using your own thinking and creativity in the process.

GETTING SERIOUS ABOUT SCHOOL

I know that some students can get through school without too much effort, just coasting through. That may be an indicator of the way they get through the rest of their life, coasting, not ever reaching their potential of greatness.

OR

You can get serious about school.

That is what this book is all about. No matter what your grade level is, or what your IQ is, if you follow the advice in this book, you will have the tools for the best foundation for learning and getting the most out of your classes.

Some students have very high intelligence and yet they don't do well in school. Something is missing.

Do you know a student like that?

Learning to be responsible for your own actions and using common sense play big parts in our everyday academic life. The fact that you are reading this is a sign that you are ready to get serious and make some changes, so let's get started!

If you do one of the things in this book, you will improve your success at school. The more things you do, the more successful you will be.

The choice is up to you.

Over the years I have helped thousands of students to be more successful. I have taken careful notes, and the issues are all the same.

Whether you are in public school or private school, I guarantee if you follow this book you will be learning to the best of your ability.

HOW TO USE THIS BOOK

This book contains two sections.

One is for parents and one is for students.

It is helpful for parents to read both sections.

The parent section is written in an easy-to-understand format. It is best utilized by reading a section and then discussing it with your student and explaining the importance of each one.

In the student section, there are easy-to-follow, simple actions that make a huge difference in class. Each one is important and, when all are used together, they will change your student's academic life.

PARENTS START HERE

You are the boss of your home.

Your student is not.

You are the role model.

You encourage.

You give the praise.

You are confident and hold to your house rules.

You are responsible for teaching your student how to become a better citizen.

You always have the final word.

WORRY-FREE ZONE
(parents)

You will have peace of mind when you know your students are learning to the best of their potential.

Let's face it, your student doesn't have to have straight A's. The important thing is that he or she is giving 100% of his or her effort.

Many parents and students just don't know how to utilize their time and resources to the best of their ability.

Learning this alone will be helpful in every area of life.

Parents, you have the most important job in the world: being role models and helping your child be a responsible, caring, and contributing citizen of the world.

Whether your student is a senior in high school or a preschooler, whether he or she is at the beginning of the semester or the end of the semester, this book will help you immeasurably.

Let's begin.

LEARNING BEGINS AT HOME GETTING ORGANIZED

The first thing we need to do is **get organized**.

It is essential that you have a monthly plan for your student. It must include all important school dates for every class, and personal and family dates as well. Do not leave any part of this to memory; it must be written down. How many of you use lists to get through the day? I write down a new list every night before bed, and then, when I get up, I look at the list and start prioritizing my day. I have not met the student yet that has the memory to remember every important class date and homework assignment without writing it down, and once students have written it down, they usually lose the paper. My calendar method is foolproof and easy' so let's get started.

You will need two blank monthly calendars.

They can be any calendar you have, but they must

be monthly calendars with blank squares that you can write in. (If you are online, you may print the calendar pages for free from my Web site).

One calendar will be for the parents and one for the student. Put the parent calendar up on the refrigerator door or other place where you and your student will see it every day.

The other calendar goes in the student's room.

The earlier students learn to utilize a calendar and write down dates, etc., the better prepared they will be for the rest of their life.

Next get your student's school calendar. Every school has a semester or quarterly calendar of school events and school holidays. This is very important. You can find one in the school office, and also online for each school.

If you have not introduced yourself to the personnel at the school office, now is the perfect time to do it.

Now write down all school holidays, vacations, start dates, and other important dates in both calendars. This will prove to be an invaluable help when planning appointments, vacations, trips, etc.

Your schedule should evolve around this school calendar. Other things that will go in this calendar are syllabus dates from each class (we will discuss the syllabus next) as well as doctors' appointments, dental appointments, work schedules, and all other important dates you need to remember.

As your student gets homework assignments each day, have them write the assignments in both calendars as soon as they get home. Make that a priority before they forget them.

Let's say for example they get an assignment for a term paper that is due in 2 weeks. Write that due date down and plan on finishing the assignment a couple days ahead of time. That allows time to work out any problems that may arise, and also the option to show the teacher an outline for approval. Most teachers will be happy to go over an outline and give advice if it is well before the due date.

SYLLABUS

The syllabus is your "bible" for each class.

Every teacher in elementary, junior high, high school, and college provides a syllabus of his or her class.

This is usually handed out the first or second day of class. Be sure your student brings home his or her syllabus from each class, and make two copies of each syllabus. (Sometimes you can find copies of the syllabus online at the school's site.)

Make a copy of each one for yourself, and have your student keep his or her copy taped to his or her study place at home.

Have a quiet time with your student with no interruptions (TV, music, phone, etc.) to go over the entire syllabus with your student.

All syllabuses are different, but most contain the same information about the class and how to contact the teacher.

Information included in the syllabus is critical to passing that class and tells you what that teacher is looking for in a successful student.

The following information is usually contained in a class syllabus.

textbook
tells the name of the textbook used in the class

study guides
tells the names of any study guides the student may need in the class

test dates
tells the dates of the tests in the class and includes the midterm and final exam dates

major homework due dates
states the due dates for major homework and daily homework expectations

project due dates
states the due dates for any projects in the class

holidays
lists all holidays for the semester, including national holidays as well as specific local school holidays

deadlines
lists all deadlines for the class

materials
lists any extra materials the student will need for the class.

class behavior expectations
explains the teacher's expectations for student behavior—what do to if the student is late, talking out of turn, cell phones, iPods, bathroom policy, what to do if your student needs to leave class early, etc.

contact information
how to contact the teacher; for example, there may be an e-mail address, phone number, and/or office hours that you may call to schedule a meeting

grading policy
explains how much value is placed on each part of the class. This may include tests, homework, attendance, quizzes, classroom behavior, projects, and participation. It tells what is expected to receive an:

A

B

C

D

F

absence policy
explains what the teacher expects the student to do (i.e.: call in, bring a note from home upon return, doctor's note, etc.) if he or she is absent because of illness or other unavoidable circumstances; some teachers allow students to make up missed tests, homework, and other assignments if they have an **excused** absence

makeup policy
explains the teacher's policy on makeup work and exams (many teachers allow students to make up missed work within an allotted amount of time, usually one to three days)

It is always frustrating to me when students come in the last week of the semester asking if they can make up assignments from months before.

It is equally frustrating when parents call me to see why their student is not doing well in class, and I explain the reason, and they are unfamiliar with the classroom policies.

This tells me the student and parent have not read the syllabus or did not understand it.

In my classes I send home a syllabus the first or second day of class after I have gone over it with the students. I attach a signature page at the end for the parents to sign acknowledging that they have read and understand the syllabus and class expectations.

The parents and student keep the syllabus at home and just return the signature page acknowledging they have read and agreed to my class policies.

It seems that many parents sign the signature page but don't take the time to read it, while others never see it because the student signs it for them, not wanting to bother them. In either case, the student and parent are not getting the full benefit from the class.

Parent **must** take an active interest in the syllabus and go over it with the students. If you don't get one within the first few days of class, be sure and ask for it!

Once you have gone over the entire syllabus, get out your two calendars.

Now copy all the important dates from each syllabus onto the calendar Have your student do the same. Also include the information for family events, birthdays, holidays, and all other important dates.

Tape one calendar on the refrigerator where it can be easily seen, and have the student tape the other calendar in his or her room in a prominent space where it will be read every day.

Make a plan with your student and discuss your expectations for his or her behavior in school and at home. Let your children know that homework *must* be done as soon as they get home from school, unless they stay at the library to do their homework.

No exceptions.

If you are at work when your children get home from school, check their homework every day when you get home. Make sure that it is complete and that they have done the right assignments.

MEETING THE TEACHER

This next step takes some extra effort but will be extremely helpful.

Within the first weeks of school, make an appointment for you and your student to have a short meeting with each teacher.

These meetings might last ten to twenty minutes and will show the teachers that you are truly concerned about your student's success in their classes.

In your first meeting, you want to tell the teacher you are a concerned parent and want to know if the teacher has any advice that could help your student be more successful in the class. Make sure the teacher knows you have read the syllabus, and ask questions about anything you might not understand.

I don't know any teacher that doesn't appreciate parents introducing themselves and saying a kind word.

It's sort of like being nice to the boss, only you will reap much bigger benefits! The more you get to know your student's teachers, the more the teachers will get to know you and your student.

This is a tremendous advantage to all concerned.

Practice introducing yourself at home to the teacher. Have your student help you pronounce the teacher's name correctly.

You can even role play with your students and spouse and relatives. The more you role play, the more comfortable you will become.

When your students see you introducing yourself at school, they will immediately become more comfortable and participate more in class. They will be more apt to ask questions and to talk to the teacher after class. They will be happy that you are a concerned parent!

Now you have started a relationship between the teacher, your student, and yourself. If there are any concerns in the future, it will be much easier to communicate with the teacher and also easier for the teacher to communicate with you. This is essential.

These early teacher meetings will positively change your and your student's life for the rest of the semester!

Every single day after school, find a time to talk to your children about their day at school and their assignments, and monitor their progress with any homework.

If you do this every day and your student comes to expect your participation, you will be amazed how much easier it will become.

Soon you will spend much less time checking homework and more time having quality conversations with your student.

Both you and your student will become much better communicators, not only in your own family, but also in school. This will ultimately lead to better communication skills he or she can use the rest of his or her life.

Good communication is absolutely essential in every aspect of our lives.

HOMEWORK THE DREADED *"H"* WORD

When most kids hear the word "homework," immediately a fear runs through them as if they had just heard the dentist's drill!

Homework is something that is not going to go away and actually helps us prepare for the real world.

With regular practice and following the steps provided in this book, the fear of homework will go away, and it will become a natural part of coming home from school.

Successful study habits will help your students establish countless beneficial patterns, from basic tasks to goal setting, that they will use the rest of their lives. The sooner they start, the easier the rest of their life will be.

CREATE A SPACE FOR STUDY

Whether your student has his or her own room or you live in a crowded apartment, create one area that is just for study. Have the student make sure to keep it in order. It is difficult to study in a cluttered, unorganized space.

It needs good light and quiet, with no distractions.

If your students have their own rooms, keep the door open while they study.

Now here are the keys:

NO MUSIC *
NO TELEVISION
NO PHONE
NO COMPUTER
NO DISTRACTIONS
during homework time.

Once your students are successful in class, you may allow them to listen to music while studying. Be sure to monitor their grades if you permit music.

I hear so many students saying they can't study without their earpods and music.

The fact is, all learners will be more productive and more receptive to remembering material if studying is done in quiet. Period.

Students cannot study effectively when they have to babysit, answer phones, cook dinner, or do other household chores.

I am not saying that students should not share in household responsibilities.

I am saying that homework *must* come first, with no distractions.

Many homework assignments can be finished in an hour or two if there are no distractions, and much of the time in less than an hour.

Sometimes the teacher will devote some class time for doing tomorrow's homework. When this happens, your students need to use that time wisely and actually do the homework.

This is perfect, because if there is a part of the homework they are having a problem with, they can ask the teacher while still in class.

If there is no place at home that is quiet, maybe your student can stay after school at the library and do his or her homework. If this is your plan, have someone—a teacher, an aide, the librarian—monitor that the student is actually doing homework and not socializing.

If the school library is not an option, find another place for the student to study quietly and do his or her homework. Make sure someone is monitoring him or her.

After a while, when students realize the benefits of having their assignments completed on time, they will enjoy getting it done and out of the way, and you will not have to monitor them.

While your students are doing their homework, make sure other siblings or family members are not being a distraction.

If you are home with your students, find something constructive that you can do at the same time. **Remember, you are your students' role model.**

You should not be watching TV or talking on the phone where your students can hear you while they are studying.

Always check your students' homework once they are finished.

Even if you don't understand how to do the problems, **you can make sure they have done the right assignment, answered the correct question numbers, read the correct chapter, etc.**

If you see mistakes, you may want to talk to your students about them, but **do not do their homework for them.** Your students' mistakes often help the teacher to evaluate what areas they need to improve in.

ALWAYS START WITH PRAISE

Every day find something to praise your child for.

Whether they are five or twenty-five, your children want to please you, even if they don't show it. Praise them much more than you criticize them.

Even by finding the smallest thing that they did right and praising them, you are making a deposit in their self-esteem and self-worth.

Praise them every day and watch the transformation that occurs. Suddenly you will find things to praise them for all the time. You will both benefit from it!

Many times when I talk to students and ask them what they think would improve their performance in school, the response is the same.

"I wish my parents were more interested in what I was doing in school."

"I wish my parents had more time to spend with me."

"I wish my parents had been stricter with me about my studies and homework."

Students crave attention from their parents.

Students crave organization and fair discipline even if they don't act like it—even if they act totally rebellious to it. The more involved you are as a parent, the better chance your student has to succeed in life. That's the bottom line.

Like it or not, your role as a parent takes 110 percent of your time and effort.

The rewards will be far greater than anything you can imagine.

MORE WAYS YOU CAN BE INVOLVED IN YOUR STUDENT'S EDUCATION

VOLUNTEER, VOLUNTEER, VOLUNTEER

Now more than ever, your school needs parent volunteers. I know we are all busy working and just keeping our heads above water, but find some time that you can volunteer. Go in person and talk to the school secretary, the principal's secretary, a teacher, or the after-school coordinator. See what you can offer them.

The more you volunteer, the more connections you will make at the school.

Making connections like this is called **networking.** This "networking" process is priceless.

You will meet other parents with the same concerns as you about their students' success.

You will meet teachers, administrators, staff, aides, security, maintenance staff, etc.

Each one of these contacts is extremely important in your student's education.

This is one of the most important things you can do. Besides being a tremendous attribute for the school, you will have an opportunity to meet many teachers, coaches, counselors, administration, and school staff.

Share your experiences with other parents in the school and support your school and its staff! They work very hard.

Some part of the school needs the services you have to offer.

NETWORKING

Networking is making contacts with other people associated with your student's school.

Always be friendly with everyone you come in contact with.

Never miss an opportunity to say hi to a familiar face or friend.

Always take advantage of opportunity and introduce yourself when you see another teacher, parent, or staff member that you don't know.

These contacts will prove invaluable as your student and you progress through school.

You may see teachers or other parents not only at school, but at the grocery store, mall, restaurants, fast-food places, takeout spots, dry cleaners, gas stations, or just waiting outside school.

The more people you meet, the more informed you will be. This is always an advantage and a fun opportunity to discuss school-related events. You will be surprised how much you have in common with the other parents at your student's school.

EXTRACIRRICULAR ACTIVITIES

Extracurricular activities are those activities usually held after school hours. Among them are:

sports
theater
band
clubs
yearbook
orchestra
student council

They help develop your student's social skills and teach teamwork, good sportsmanship, responsibility, confidence building, creativity, routines, individuality, and the benefits of exercise.

Have a discussion with your students and let them know your expectations. It's great to be in a sport, but not at the expense of grades. This will usually give the student an incentive to be more successful at academics.

PARTICIPATE

It is important to attend as many games, shows, concerts, recitals, and performances that your student is involved in as possible. Whether your student has a small part, a big part, is on the starting team, or is sitting on the sidelines, showing your support by being there will make a tremendous difference. It is also a great networking opportunity.

Never sit at a game texting or conducting business on your phone or laptop.

Be enthusiastic, be supportive, be happy, and be involved in your student's life!

SCHEDULING APPOINTMENTS

Whenever possible, always schedule your student's appointments outside of school time.

Doctor's, dentist's and other necessary appointments should always be made after school or on non-school days.

Usually the appointment staff understands and will find you an appointment away from school time.

There are also many Mondays and Fridays that are school holidays but not holidays for professional medical people.

If you absolutely must schedule an appointment during a class time, take the following measures:

1. Write a legible note to the teacher explaining that this appointment is unavoidable and you hate to have your student miss class. Sign it and include a contact number.

2. Ask for any reading and homework that will be missed, and be sure your student has it done before returning to the class the next day.

3. Have your student contact a "study friend" in the class to find out anything else that may have come up during his or her absence.

4. Whenever I have a student come to class with a note saying he or she will need to leave class early for an appointment, not only does the student miss that day's lesson and homework (usually homework is based on the lesson taught in class that day), but he or she also will need to make that day up.

It is also more work for the teacher who is already on overload with larger classes.

Going back to the importance of being earnest as a student and a parent, **not scheduling appointments during school hours** is just one more thing that will help your student be more successful in class.

Please avoid this common practice, and schedule your appointments outside of school.

Teachers try to follow lesson plans closely, but, as in life, things may come up in class and cause the lesson plan to be continued the next day, or the class may move forward faster than expected and start on a new lesson plan sooner than planned.

Your role is to always be prepared and communicate.

PARENT EXCUSES AND ABSENCES

In order for your students to do their very best in each class, they must not miss one day of the entire semester. Of course, if they are truly sick, they should stay home until they are well. No teacher wants the rest of his or her students exposed to illnesses such as a cold, flu, etc. If your student is sick, keep him or her at home. Be sure that you find out any assignments or homework from another student or from the teacher.

If there is a missed exam, see if you can reschedule that exam when your student is well.

As for unexcused absences, most of the following problems can be avoided if you follow the steps in this book and plan ahead the night before.

No ride
Car won't start
Forgot homework
Lost homework
Printer out of ink
Printer broke
Alarm didn't go off

Many times I have a student that needs to miss class with a note from the parents saying their student has to go with them to place A or place B.

Again, this is sending the message both to the teacher and to the student that the student's education is not as important as the parents' agenda.

Please do not let this happen to your student. In the long run, your student will benefit in untold ways from daily attendance and making school his or her number one priority.

Make sure your student has 100 percent attendance with no tardies or partial classes.

MODELING

The way you, as parents, act has a profound influence on your children. Whether you know it or not, they are watching you and how you behave and react to everyday life.

If your life is unorganized and you are always rushing and being late, chances are that is going to become part of your students' characteristics as well.

It is very important that you organize your life so that you can help your students organize theirs.

TAKING YOUR STUDENT TO AND FROM SCHOOL

The time you spend taking your student to school is very important. It sets the tone in the morning for the student's day. If you are always rushing and stressed, the student brings that to the classroom. Plan your morning the evening before and set your alarm so you and your student have plenty of time. You will be amazed how much better your day will go, not to mention your student's day!

When school lets out for the day, most schools look like a mass "free-for-all" outside the school. Some parents will have arrived early to be first in line to pick up their students. It seems like all parking rules and driving rules are nonexistent, and many parents think they can park or act however they want. Is this scenario familiar to you?

That is why almost all schools have security, traffic guards, or teachers to help monitor the parking areas after school.

Still, every single day, cars are lined up down the street around many schools, blocking the flow of traffic. Those in the front of the line won't move until their student shows up. Cars are double parked, parked in the red zone, horns are honking, and other parents are sitting in their car blocking spaces where others need to park or need to leave a space.

Tempers are tested, and sometimes there is yelling as well as displays of frustration. This is always inappropriate. **Is this how you want your student to act when he or she starts driving?**

Instead, find an easier way. Decide on a place to meet your student ahead of time. Maybe it might be at the other side of school or on an adjacent street.

Maybe your student could study in the library for thirty minutes until all the traffic rush has subsided. This will be easier for you and for your student. It will be much easier for you to drive up to the school with no traffic to contend with. Is it possible to carpool with a neighbor?

If you must pick your student up right away, never honk your horn, yell at another parent or student or teacher, or park so as to block traffic or other parked cars.

If you see a security guard, or traffic guard, **thank him or her** for his or her presence and for helping out.

Security guards and traffic guards are part of that group of unsung school personnel that don't get thanked or appreciated enough. A kind and complimentary word from you will make a big difference and will be well appreciated.

While school is in session:

If an emergency arises or you just need to leave your student a message about being picked up after school, call the school office and ask to have your message delivered, or have your student call you at lunch or between classes.

There is no reason for your student to have his or her cell phone at school, much less have it in class. I don't know anyone that can resist looking at who a text message is from during class. Make any arrangements before school, and clear them at the office if need be. Please make every effort not to interrupt your student during school, and especially during class.

AFTER SCHOOL

Homework is the number one priority. No cell phones, iPods, TV, music, or other distractions. Do not buy into the "I can study better with music" plea, etc. Do not let your student influence this. Homework *must* be done in a quiet place with no distractions.

Once students are getting good grades, then allow them to study with music as long as they keep up their grades.

Do your homework *neatly*. If you make mistakes, erase them so you turn in a neat page.

Remember to put your name at the top of each page. I can't tell you how many assignments I get without names on them. Print your name always. If I have to spend time figuring out whose assignment it is, that might have an influence on that "gray" area of grading we talked about.

The priority after homework is chores. If there are any chores you have for your students, have them do them after the homework is done and before they do anything else.

Once the homework and chores are done, the student gets some well-deserved time of his or her own. The earlier you start doing this routine, the more your student will become accustomed to it, and it will just seem natural to do his or her homework and chores first.

Before getting ready for bed, help your students get set up for the next day by getting their clothes ready and putting their homework, books, backpack, etc., where they won't forget them the next morning.

If you need to charge your phone, do it now.

BEDTIME

Have an established bedtime on school nights and stick to it. Your student should have at least eight hours for sleep.

All electronic devices (computers, TVs, music, etc.) should be turned off an hour before bedtime.

The last hour should be spent reading or writing.

Reading can be anything the student likes to read. If your student doesn't know any books to read for pleasure, have his or her teachers recommend some outside reading, and go to the public library and check out some books.

You can find a list of recommended books by grade on my Web site:

PASSTHECLASS.ORG

By now your routine should be running smoothly. You have had your meeting with the teachers and your student.

Have your student meet with the teacher to check on his or her progress. If the student doesn't have a progress report from the teacher, or gives you an excuse, be sure to follow up and, if need be, contact the teacher yourself.

The more your student learns to do independently, the better prepared he or she will be to handle the challenges of higher education ahead.

COMMUNICATION

Communication is one of the most important skills your student can learn.

Teach your student how to meet other adults as well as students.

If you host your student's friends at your home for a birthday party, how many of your student's friends come up and introduce themselves to you and say a complimentary word? If they do, think about the favorable impression they have made on you, as opposed to the student's friend that comes to the party and just says hello or doesn't speak to you at all.

Be sure that your student acknowledges everyone in a room, especially the adults.

Teach your student how to give a firm handshake and look the person in the eyes, smile, and find something complimentary to say.

Teach him or her to always say goodbye after a meeting or party, and to thank the host.

LANGUAGE CHALLENGES

Maybe English is not your best language, or maybe you just feel awkward talking to a teacher. Let me assure you, every teacher welcomes parent communication.

Don't worry about your possible language barriers. If need be, have your student or a friend help you translate and communicate with the teacher. You will find it is easier than you think.

The teacher will appreciate the effort you are making. Let's face it, teachers *want* to help students; that's why they are teaching. The more communication you have with your student's teacher, the more you are in the know and can help your student be successful.

These are important skills that will accelerate your student forward for the rest of his or her life.

The benefits are endless, and the results and successes are staggering. Yet most students don't take advantage of them. Why? Many that are not self-starters need encouragement and guidance from their family. **Family, whether you realize it or not, is the**

most important factor in your student's life, and your participation in your student's school life is critical.

Education is not just about the goal, it is about the journey.

Soak up as much as you can.

FUNDAMENTAL TECHNIQUES OF PARENT-TEACHER COMMUNICATION

I cannot stress enough how much easier both your life and your student's life will be if you maintain a healthy communication with teachers.

Please don't be hesitant for any reason to talk to each and every one of your student's teachers. It is our job to help students complete their classes successfully, taking with them as much knowledge as possible.

I have some parents who communicate with me almost weekly.

I have many more parents that I never meet at all.

I have some parents that I meet at the end of the semester when their student's grade is in jeopardy.

It is a fair statement that I do not meet 95 percent of my students' parents.

If you feel your student is not giving or getting 100 percent, first talk to your student, then talk to the teacher.

If your student has a problem at school, be sure you become involved and understand the entire situation before passing judgment, and especially before you make any decisions about your stance. In most instances, these situations are a result of poor communication and can be resolved in a manner that is satisfactory to both the student and the teacher.

How you approach the teacher, whether you realize it or not, will influence how your student approaches teachers and other authority figures in his or her adult life, so this is a great time to show professionalism, understanding, and listening skills.

This is where you can shine at being a good role model and parent.

HOW TO START

If your student is old enough, ask him or her to set up a meeting after school with the teacher.

You may also send a note with your student to give to the teacher. Give your phone number and ask the teacher to call you to arrange a meeting at a convenient time.

Make sure that you and your student will be able to attend at the set time.

Bring a pen and paper. *Take notes!*

All of us can be forgetful. We all have different ways of remembering things if we want to be successful. (For example, I sit down each morning and take a piece of notebook paper and list my priorities for the day. I list things on my to-do list, and any extras. I also have a column for the important people in my life and anything I can do for them that day.)

Set the tone for the meeting. The first minute of any meeting will usually determine the tone for the rest of the meeting. Don't start with accusatory remarks; instead start with a compliment and a pleasant tone. Introduce yourself and shake hands. Act concerned about your student. Show the teacher that you think he or she is important in your student's future.

Here is a list of questions you might ask the teacher. At the meeting, act grateful for the meeting and be respectful. This means letting the teacher talk first. Listen and don't interrupt. If you are unsure about anything the teacher is talking about, be sure to have him or her clarify it for you.

When it is your turn to talk, be prepared. Here is a list of questions that may be helpful to ask the teacher.

1. Is my student's homework being turned in on time and complete?

2. In your opinion, is my student giving 100 percent effort in your class? If not, why?

3. How is my student's classroom behavior?

4. What are ways you would like to see my student improve?

5. How are you helping my student become successful in his or her weak areas?

6. How can I help?

Work with the teacher to activate a plan of action and schedule a follow-up.

Remember, teachers' time is limited. Please keep your meetings short (ten to fifteen minutes is usually sufficient) by having your questions written down before you go in. Have everyone in your group arrive ten minutes early. Take a paper and pen and take notes. This is very important, as everyone will hear things differently. Make sure your notes are specific. Always end with a **plan of action** for the student to take, and **schedule a follow-up** to check on the student's progress. This follow-up can be an e-mail, a phone call, or a visit.

Be sure you are directly communicating with the teacher, and thank him or her.

When you get home, help your student write and send a thank you note by mail to the teacher at the school (see the form section of my Web site for samples).

FOLLOWING UP

Following up is exactly that.

After you have a teacher meeting, whether by phone or in person, and make a schedule of what your student needs to do to make up homework, a test, or other project, be sure to **follow up** and make sure that it is done in a timely manner exactly as you had discussed with the teacher.

If you have gotten this far, *congratulations!*

You are well on your way to helping your student be successful in school.

Please have a friendly family meeting with you and your student. Plan it ahead of time so everyone can be there.

Now go back and evaluate how you are doing. What are the things that have worked best for you? What are the things you might want to improve upon or change?

What about your student? Ask for his or her honest opinion of what is working for him or her.

Explain again how important education is to the rest of your student's life, and most students will be honest with you. Students know if you are sincere. Even though they may pretend not to know what is going on or why they can't do well in school, down inside they do know and want to talk about it.

THINGS YOU CAN PRACTICE AT HOME

The following are things you can practice with your student at home that will help him or her immeasurably at school.

PUBLIC SPEAKING

Talking in front of the class or a group of people is a learned skill. After you do it long enough, it becomes second nature. Although some people are never truly comfortable giving speeches or talking in front of others, the more you practice it and the younger you start, the easier it will be.

Start out by having your student stand up and read a report he or she has done to you or your family. It's OK to start with something easy and short. The important thing is to just get comfortable doing it.

Very important: Never laugh, ridicule, or diminish the importance of your student's talk. Even if he or she made mistakes, find something positive your student did or said to compliment him or her on. This will reinforce your student's confidence tremendously when speaking in public.

After your student has finished reading a book, whether for school, or just for pleasure, have him or her write a book report and practice reading it in front of a mirror in his or her room.

Talking to yourself in front of a mirror is a good place to evaluate your posture, hand gestures, and speaking manner.

Then have the student give a book presentation to you. At the beginning it might be short, just a few minutes. After he or she gets comfortable doing this, the reports will get longer, and your student will actually enjoy performing for you and having your attention.

Many families now have access to recording a video, whether it be on their cell phones, a digital camera or a video camera. Utilize this great learning tool and record your student speaking. Then show it to the student and point out the good qualities. The student will see what he or she needs to practice on. Visual aids such as this that you can do at home are fantastic learning tools!

As students grow and gain more confidence, their reports will get longer and their comfort level will be much greater.

This is invaluable experience that they will carry with them the rest of their lives.

THINGS PARENTS CAN DO EVERYDAY

1. Make sure your student is prepared the night before school (checklist on page)

2. Have your student eat something healthy for breakfast, like oatmeal and juice or even a banana and whole-grain muffin.

3. Praise your student for something every day.

4. Show gratitude for the effort your student is giving in school.

5. Thank your student for any helpful things he or she does around the house.

6. Make sure your student brushes his or her teeth after meals and flosses before bed.

7. Check your student's appearance every day before school.

8. Show trust in your student until he or she proves otherwise.

9. Be a positive example for your student in every aspect of your life.

10. Know what your student is doing online.

11. Know your student's whereabouts, friends, and how to reach your student at all times.

INTERNET

The Internet is a fantastic place for learning. It can also be a fantastic place for your student to spend countless hours on games or social networking sites instead of doing productive things.

Most students need to be supervised while online if they are under sixteen years old.

If you, as a parent, allow them on a social networking site, you need to be responsible for their behavior there.

If your son or daughter is on one of those sites, randomly check his or her profile and friends network.

Discuss what is appropriate for your family and what you feel comfortable with.

You need to have house rules about computer use and stick to them.

EARNING PRIVILEGES

Just as we adults earn privileges by working and getting paid, students need to earn their privileges, too.

If you don't feel your student is giving 100 percent effort to his or her studies, then you can limit the student's online privileges, TV watching, video game playing, or other things he or she enjoys.

Sit down with your family and decide what needs to happen to earn more privileges.

Certainly if your student is up on the computer until 2 a.m. on school nights, he or she will not be very receptive to learning the following day. Set guidelines that are appropriate for your family and stick to them.

An example might be music. Once students are following the advice in this book and are more successful in class, they earn back the privilege of listening to music while studying as long as they keep their grades up.

If students know their boundaries and what they need to do to earn more privileges, it becomes automatic, not unlike driving a car and having to follow traffic rules.

Students will be more apt to put forth effort if they see a benefit.

Student accountability is a big step towards successful learning.

HOW WELL DO YOU KNOW YOUR STUDENT?

Involve yourself in your student's world.

Being interested in your student's world is the most helpful and satisfying thing you can do to gain your student's respect and love.

Can you answer the following questions about your student?

1. What is your student's favorite movie?

2. Who is his or her favorite singer?

3. What's his or her favorite song? have you ever listened to the lyrics?

4. What's your student's favorite class?

5. Who is his or her favorite teacher? Why?

6. What's your student's favorite food?

7. What does he or she like to do in their spare time?

8. Who are your student's friends? Have you met and talked with them?

9. What are your student's goals and aspirations?

If you don't know the answer to these questions, start spending more quality time with your student. He or she will love you for it.

KEEPING A JOURNAL
(for parents)

Many people find it extremely helpful to keep a journal.

This is merely getting a notebook and writing down your thoughts about the day every night before bed.

What did you do that you were proud of?

What happened in your family that was good?

It really doesn't matter how long you write, just that you write. You may start with just a paragraph and find out in a few weeks you are writing a couple of pages.

Before long you will be excited about journaling each night. You will be able to go back a year from now and read your journal and see how much your life has changed for the better!

PERSISTENCE

If there is one thing we as parents must demonstrate to our students, it is that we are as serious as we say. If we talk the talk, we must also walk the walk.

Persistence simply means that we **consistently** spend time with our children talking about what they are learning in school and making sure that they are 100 percent prepared the night before school for the next day.

When your student leaves for school in the morning, being prepared will relieve his or her stress, help him or her get a better night's sleep, and ensure that he or she arrives at school ready to learn and eager to share.

You'll be surprised how just a little time spent on prep-aration the night before will relieve a lot of your stress also!

STUDENT SECTION

(FOR PARENTS ALSO)

FOR STUDENTS

I have had the idea of writing this book for many years. Every time I start a new semester, have a student conference, or communicate with parents, I can see tremendous ways I, as a teacher, can help.

I have never met a parent that didn't want to help his or her child in school, and I have never met a child that didn't want to impress his or her parents. Yet they lack some knowledge, so simple yet so basic, that will easily help them be successful.

So, my book idea was basically intended for students. As I wrote ideas and took notes, I realized that this book should be as much for parents as it is for students. Your parents are your role models for your formative years as well as your school years. So no matter what year you start the principles of this book, whether it be elementary, intermediate, or high school, you will see immediate, fantastic results !

Each of you has the potential for greatness. Whether your parent is involved with your academic life or not, you cannot afford to take education lightly.

Appearance, behavior, and enthusiasm all contribute to your overall experience at school and will make a 100 percent difference.

There are more distractions for students than ever before. You are being bombarded with all types of media and marketing. Do not let this get in the way of your education.

Take the grade you are in and subtract it from twelve. That is the number of school years you have left.

With college and trade schools becoming more and more difficult to get into, you want to be as successful as possible now. These next chapters are for you. I encourage you to read them and take them seriously. It really will make a difference.

It is the foundation for the rest of your life!

HOW TO USE THIS BOOK
(students)

All of us can be more successful at whatever we do if we have enthusiasm and the right tools.

The tools you need to be successful in school are here in this book. All you have to do is follow them.

If you use one thing, you will improve from where you are now.

If you use two things, you will improve even more.

When you use all the tools in this book, you will be 100 percent more successful than you are now.

Try it!

WORRY-FREE ZONE
(the time between when homework, studying,
and chores are done and bedtime)

If you read this book and follow each simple principle, you will improve in school 100 percent.

The amount you improve directly correlates to the amount of your effort.

You will not only have a fantastic school experience, you will also have much better relationships at home.

Your school social life will improve.

You will feel good that you have tried to the best of your ability.

When you become a parent, you will already know how to guide your children on a lifelong plan for success.

ON BEING SUCCESSFUL

Being successful in school is no different than being successful at anything else.

To lose weight, diet and exercise are the only ways.

To save money, you must organize, plan, and spend wisely.

To get a driver's license, practice, study the rules, review, take the test, pass, and drive.

To get through school, organize, study, focus, stick to the calendar, and give 100 percent effort.

PASS THE CLASS!

FIRST IMPRESSIONS

First impressions matter. **Most people form an opinion of you before you even speak**.

Just by your appearance, you are making an impression on people whether you realize it or not.

Even in job interviews, the interviewer forms an impression of the interviewee just by the way he or she looks. Research tells us that most employers know whether they want to hire someone within the first few minutes of the interview based solely on their first impression.

Appearance, body language, and attitude all make up a first impression.

Have you ever formed an opinion of someone based on the way he or she looks and later changed your opinion after you got to know the person? Sure, we all have.

That first impression is so important; we want it to be a good one!

No matter what grade you are in, your appearance is very important.

No matter what your background is, your appearance speaks very loudly and can affect the way you act in class.

If your appearance is less than your best, do not expect to be taken very seriously at school.

For girls and guys, the following appearance guidelines will make a difference:

1. Hygiene: Take a shower every day, wear deodorant, and brush and floss your teeth before school. Do not wear perfume or cologne. Perfumes and colognes are for evening or special occasions and should not be worn to school.

Make sure your breath is fresh. If you take good care of your teeth and have a healthy diet, you will always have fresh breath. Be sure and brush your teeth and floss every night before you go to bed. If you can, take a toothbrush to school with you and brush after lunch. You will not be embarrassed in class when someone says you have food stuck in your teeth, and you will benefit from healthy teeth and gums and fewer trips to the dentist.

2. Hair: Your hair should be clean and away from your eyes and face. If you like to wear your hair long, be sure it looks clean and brushed. The length of your hair is not as important as making sure it looks like you take care of it. If you get up in the morning and rush to school, it will look as if you don't care about your appearance, which in turn affects the rest of your appearance.

Shoes: Your shoes reflect the entire rest of your appearance. Be sure they are shined and clean. If you take good care of your shoes they will last much longer.

ADVICE FOR GUYS:

Wear comfortable-fitting jeans or pants that require a belt at the waist. Make sure your jeans are in good shape. No holes or rips.

If you join the trend of wearing your pants below your buttocks and letting your boxers show, take a good look at yourself in the mirror and re-evaluate your appearance. This book isn't about being popular in school; it's about being more successful in school, and your future success in life.

Keep your shoelaces tied.

Some schools require that you tuck your shirt in.

Your school's dress code will mandate the way you can dress. If you walk around with your jeans around your thighs, you probably won't be taken as seriously by adults, who ultimately have the final say in your grades and promotions and referrals. Before you leave the house each day, look in the mirror and evaluate your appearance. Do your clothes look clean and fit well? Is your hair clean? Teeth brushed? Do you look healthy?

ADVICE FOR GIRLS:

Wear clothes you are comfortable in. Do not wear low-cut tops and dresses or too-short shorts to school. This might send the wrong message. You are at school to learn and should dress appropriately. You should not wear inappropriate clothes to school. Save those clothes for parties or special occasions, but do not wear them to school.

Your hair should be clean.

Do not wear a lot of makeup to school. This may sound old-fashioned, but remember, this book is about getting you ahead in school, so please take my advice here.

Most of the girls I see at school take pride in their appearance and always look clean and fresh. Some girls try to look much older than they are. Save those looks for other occasions. Use school as an opportunity to learn.

GETTING READY FOR SCHOOL

The night before school, lay out the clothes you are going to wear the next day.

Make sure they look clean and fit well.

Make sure your shoes are in good repair and polished. If you are wearing tennis shoes or sneakers, be sure they look clean.

Have your underwear, belt, socks, shoes, jacket, etc. all in place so in the morning, all you have to do is wash, do your hair, dress, eat breakfast, and brush your teeth.

Have your books, homework, pen, paper, backpack, and snack by the door in one place so you do not forget to take anything to school.

This will greatly reduce your stress in the morning and actually help you sleep better the night before without having to worry about forgetting anything when you get up.

I don't think a day goes by in my classroom without at least one student forgetting his or her homework or assignment.

I get excuses like:

I left it in the car.
I forgot it at home.
The dog ate it.
It flew out the window of the car on the way to school.
My mom will bring it after school
Someone stole it.
My brother spilled on it.
I lost it.

While some of these may be true, the bottom line is you are not prepared for class, and because of you the entire class will have to slow down and may not get everything done today as planned.

Take responsibility for yourself and come to class prepared and ready to learn. In every class, there is always one person who thinks it's funny to come unprepared and create commotion or attention. Don't be that person. It slows down the entire class.

TALKING DURING CLASS

If there is one thing that slows down my lesson plan and bothers most teachers more than anything else, it is talking inappropriately during class.

Just because the teacher is looking the other way or has given you an assignment to work on, it doesn't mean you may talk to your neighbor.

In almost every case, the students that are talking are the students that need to be studying the most.

If you want to be more successful in a class, don't talk unless you raise your hand, or unless the teacher says it's ok to talk.

Stay focused during class. Save your visiting until after class.

CLASSROOM LAYOUT

Most students don't notice classroom layout. When you enter your classroom, take a few minutes before class to look around. Usually the teacher's desk is in the front of the class. I always arrange my classroom so my desk is in the back and the podium and white-board are in the front, with the students facing the front. Sometimes it just depends on the space in the classroom and number of desks in the room. There may be tables instead of desks. If you sit at a table, try to sit up front at one of the ends towards the center. This way you will only have a student on one side instead of two.

Look at the walls. Are there pictures or graphs or posters? Teachers try to decorate their classrooms to interest the students in the subject being taught. What are the pictures of? Usually you can get an idea of the teacher's personality by the way he or she decorates the classroom. It might be serious, it might be educational, it might be fun, or there might be personal pictures that the teacher has taken of places he or she has visited.

If you want to help the teacher form a good impression of you, ask the teacher about some of the things on the wall. Of course, you should do this before or after class—never after the teacher has started the lesson. Maybe one of the pictures is of somewhere you have been, or somewhere you want to visit in the future. Share that with the teacher. It will start a communication with the teacher. As previously mentioned, the more you communicate with the teacher, the more you are showing that you are a committed and interested student. There might be a city or place you don't know. Ask about it. Listen to the teacher's story about it and show interest. If you run out of things to say, you can always ask "Who, what, where, when, and why?" Teachers love students that show interest. Be enthusiastic. Many students sit through an entire semester and cannot describe what is on the walls of their classroom. Can you?

CLASSROOM ETIQUETTE

On the first day of a new class, be sure to find out what the classroom etiquette is and then follow it. What do you do if you need to use the bathroom? Is there a pencil sharpener? What about Scotch tape, paper clips, a stapler, extra paper? What is off limits? In my classroom I keep all the above supplies in a specific location and tell students they may use them when they need to.

My desk drawers are off limits to students. I do not like to find students going through my desk or looking at my school laptop or grade book without my permission. There is a lot of student information that should not be seen by other students, such as grades, phone numbers, comments, etc. I make sure to tell students this. Just as students would not want the teacher to go through their computer, backpack, or other personal items, it becomes a lesson in mutual respect.

Do you need a bathroom key to use the bathrooms? Does the teacher require you to raise your hand and ask to use the restroom, or can you just get up and use it? Always go to the restroom alone. There is seldom a reason to take a friend to the restroom with you. This can make the teacher suspicious of why you are going to the restroom. Try and use the restroom on your break between classes. That's what breaks are for. If you have a long class and have a break, use it then. It is frustrating to the teacher to give a break and as soon as the break is over and the teacher starts the lesson, a student wants to use the restroom or get a drink.

I have a three-hour class in the evening and give a ten-minute break at an appropriate time about halfway. Almost every day as soon as we get back from break and start on the lesson, a hand will go up and someone will need to use the restroom.

What did the student do during the ten-minute break? Usually spend his or her time texting or talking to friends.

Of course, if it is an emergency, any teacher will not mind you using the restroom when you need to.

If it happens every day right after your break, it will affect your "student image." Your student image is how the teachers and staff perceive you. Do they perceive you as a student that is there because he or she is interested in class and eager to learn, or do they perceive you as a student who is there for credits? Your student image will follow you for your entire student year. First impressions are hard to change, so make sure yours is a good one.

ATTITUDE

Your attitude is probably the biggest trait that will help you get through school (and life!).

If you go to class with a good attitude every day, you are going to be much more receptive to learning.

Also, the teacher will notice your good attitude and, at the end of the day, that attitude will get you those "unrecorded" marks that can make or break your grade.

Go to school with a positive attitude every day and a smile on your face. These will be some of the best memories you will have!

BODY LANGUAGE

Your teachers read your body language before they ever hear you speak.

It can scream at someone just by the way you walk and carry yourself.

When speaking to another person, never have your arms crossed. Keep them in an open position to show the person you are speaking to that you are receptive to their ideas.

Before ever starting to speak to another person, make sure your body language is friendly, and always look others in the eyes with a pleasant expression.

GOAL SETTING

Goal setting is a very helpful tool both in school and in life. Goal setting means thinking about the outcome you want to have and setting goals to achieve along the way.

Start with short-term goals. Write them down. Get out your calendar that we discussed in the first section and mark down one goal.

For example, if you have a term paper due on a certain date, write down a goal of finishing the paper several days before the due date. Then tell the teacher you have worked hard on this paper and ask if there is a time he could review it with you and give you any advice on how to improve it, or just make sure you are on track with what the teacher is looking for. Most teachers will be happy to do this provided you do it well before the due date.

An Example of Goal Setting:

Your English teacher assigns a research paper that is due in three weeks.

If the paper is due in three weeks, your goals might look like this:

Day 1

Jot down your ideas immediately after you get home while the assignment is still fresh in your mind.

End of week 1

Have your basic outline written down, and the theme of your paper. Do all your research and organize it the way you will write it in the paper. You might even try to meet with the teacher after class briefly and have him or her OK your outline.

End of week 2

Write your paper and check for spelling, punctuation, grammar, etc.

Now have someone proofread if for you. When you are satisfied with the results, ask the teacher if you could see him or her briefly to go over your subject and rough outline. Often times the teacher may give you some input that you haven't thought of to improve your paper. At the very least, he or she will know that you are working on it and not procrastinating until the last minute.

Type the final draft.

Look the paper over.

Does it look neat? If you can't read it or understand it, redo it. The teacher doesn't have time to try and decode your paper, so make sure it is legible.

Correct any typos and misspellings.

Would you give the paper an A grade? If you don't think it's an A paper, no one else is going to either.

Always make a copy for yourself and keep it in your file.

Week 3

Make sure you turn in your paper the exact way the teacher wants it submitted. It may be in a folder, typed and stapled, printed, handwritten. etc. If the teacher asks for it typed, do not turn it in handwritten with an excuse. If the teacher accepts the paper early, turn it in early. Otherwise don't jeopardize your grade by turning in the paper late. Be sure to turn it in on time.

MANNERS MATTER

Whether you realize it or not, people are watching you throughout the day, forming impressions based on your appearance and actions.

Be sure and practice good manners.

Be polite.

Always address adults by a courtesy title and their last name (i.e.: Mr. Smith, Mrs. Garcia) until they tell you otherwise.

Follow the golden rule.

Be sure you know how to conduct yourself properly in special situations. If you're not sure, ask your parents or teacher.

Don't brush your hair in public places, such as the classroom or cafeteria. Although everyone likes that you have pretty hair, not everyone appreciates the stuff that flies out of your hair when you brush it near them.

Always use "please" and "thank you."

HOW TO TALK TO AN ADULT

Always acknowledge other people in the room. If you go to a friend's house, don't wait to be introduced to the parents or other adults. Go up and introduce yourself very politely.

Follow these tips:

Speak clearly.
Be enthusiastic about meeting them.
Have a firm handshake.
Look them in the eyes when talking to them.
Smile.
Find something complimentary to say to them.
When you leave the room, be sure and say good-bye, and thank them if appropriate.

For other tips on manners, please see the Web site:

PASSTHECLASS.ORG

VOLUNTEER

A very rewarding part of life that many students don't take advantage of is **volunteering**.

Volunteering is a great way to meet new people, feel good about yourself, and contribute to the good energy of the planet.

There are many opportunities to volunteer at school. If you can't think of any, ask your teacher, coach, or counselor. Sometimes teachers appreciate a student who volunteers to clean the whiteboard or blackboard, straighten the chairs, or put the books in order. All these little things will also give you some time to talk to the teacher, who will have an entirely new impression of you if you haven't done it before. Try it!

You can also volunteer in your church, your community center, or your neighborhood. Maybe there is a younger student that you could help with his or her homework and serve as a mentor?

Volunteering provides excellent networking skills and a great feeling of helping someone else.

NETWORKING

Always greet and meet new people that you come in contact with.

Make an effort to learn everyone's name in your class.

Expect the best from your teachers. They are there to help. If you think the teacher isn't fair, talk to the teacher and make notes. If nothing changes, then talk to your parents and make an appointment with the teacher.

If this doesn't solve the issue, make an appointment with your counselor or the principal. Don't go through an entire semester feeling that your teacher isn't fair. It more than likely is a communication problem that can be solved if you meet with the teacher and tell him or her your feelings. Always use a pleasant tone and good manners.

STUDY PARTNER

It is important to find a study partner for each of your classes. Make sure it is a student who is responsible and you have a good rapport with.

Trade phone numbers and e-mail addresses with your partner. He or she will be your backup in case of any questions or absences you may have.

If you are not sure of a problem or assignment, call your study partner to confirm the assignment or get some helpful insight to the problem.

Alternately, he or she can call you for the same issues.

This is another reason why it is important to do your homework as soon as you get home.

This way you have time to talk to your study partner about any issues from class.

IF YOU MUST MISS A CLASS

If you must miss a class, be sure and communicate with the teacher *before* the missed class. A note from your parent, or a call, will usually suffice.

Ask if there are any assignments you can do while you are gone, and be sure and do them.

EXTRA CREDIT

If you are behind in a class or just starting on your new tools that you have learned in this book, you might consider asking the teacher for an extra - credit assignment. Not all teachers will have an extra-credit assignment.

It is important not to wait until the last weeks of school when you are doing poorly to ask for extra credit. The teacher is more likely to give it earlier in the semester when your grade is not heavily dependent upon the extra credit.

PRAISE

Everyone loves to be complimented, especially for something he or she worked at. Your teacher is no exception. If you think a teacher did something special or did something that helped you learn something new, be sure to tell him or her after class. Even if you have to rush to get to your next class, take the time to go up and tell the teacher what you liked about the lesson. The teacher will love the compliment and also like the fact that you took the time to give a compliment.

In the same manner, if you are at a restaurant and have a good waitress or waiter, be sure and compliment them to the manager or owner. We all hear far too many complaints and too few compliments.

You will be amazed how good you feel when you praise someone else or give another person a compliment.

Give a compliment when you really mean it and expect nothing in return for it. Look for things that are right. Give compliments to your teachers, counselors, coaches, classmates, lunch staff, friends.

Most of all, show appreciation to your parents and family members. Remember, your parents are doing the very best they know how to make a better life for you. Find time to do something special for them. Do some yard work or clean your room without being asked. Make your bed every day and keep your laundry up. You will be amazed how much better your life will be. The rewards are endless.

Try doing this for a month, and I guarantee you will see a change in your life for the better.

Try it!

THINGS YOU CAN DO TODAY THAT WILL INSTANTLY IMPROVE YOUR PERFORMANCE AT SCHOOL

1. Be there on time and seated.

2. Sit up front

3. Pay attention. Take notes.

4. Participate.

5. Ask questions.

6. Don't be the first one out the door.

7. Sit up front; don't sit with a friend.

8. No cell phones, iPods, etc.

9. Be 100 percent ready for every class.

10. Clean up after yourself.

11. Be the most polite person in the room.

EFFORT

Remember, the effort you put into school will exactly parallel the results your get back.

If you don't study or if you wait to do a paper until the last minute, don't expect to receive a very good grade.

You may think you can fool the teacher, but teachers have been around a lot longer than you. Remember, we were students once also. If I am grading sixty papers on the same subject, I can immediately tell the papers that were done at the last minute or that were borrowed from the Internet.

Try the advice in this book and you will be amazed how much easier school and life will become.

PROCRASTINATION

If there is one habit I could pick out that is universally typical of most students, it is procrastination.

Procrastination is putting something off that you don't want to do until the last minute.

How many of you do that? Most of us do it to some extent.

Most adults have learned that it's easier in the long run not to procrastinate.

If you procrastinate about your homework and you end up having a question, usually, by the time you get to it, it's too late to call someone for help or for the information you need.

FUNDAMENTAL TECHNIQUES OF SUCCESS IN MODERN EDUCATION

1. Be early to class.

2. When you arrive in class, check the board for any instructions.

3. Have your homework out and ready to turn in. with your name on it. Don't lose your homework .

4. Have your book open and be reviewing when the bell rings.

5. *Always* have a paper and pencil.

6. If you need to use the restroom, do it before class starts.

7. Take legible notes that anyone can read.

8. No iPods, cell phones, headphones, etc., in the classroom.

9. Participate.

10. Ask questions.

11. Get excited about the subject.

12. Never talk at inappropriate times, and don't ridicule another student's answer.

13. Treat your classmates as a team.

14. Give positive feedback to your classmates and teacher.

15. Always address elders by their last name unless they tell you otherwise.

16. Don't brush your hair in public.

17. Use "please" and "thank you."

18. At a meeting, always acknowledge everyone in the room.

19. Be the most polite one in the room.

20. Never be the first one out of the classroom.

21. Don't depend on another student's word about a change of assignment date.

22. Practice complimenting at least two people a day.

23. Be aware of everything around you without being noticed.

24. Do your homework and chores without being told.

25. Think the best, expect the best.

26. Volunteer.

27. Hang out with students that are successful in school.

28. Do not leave class without understanding the homework assignment and writing it down.

29. **Practice not saying or doing anything negative for a whole day.**

30. Do something kind for someone else and don't expect anything in return.

MEET THE TEACHER

Meeting the teacher for a one-to-one meeting is one of the most important things you can do to be successful in his or her class, yet very few students do it.

Go up after class and ask the teacher when you may schedule a short meeting with him or her.

Then be sure and follow through.

At the meeting, tell the teacher your goals and ask if there is any advice he or she can give you.

Ask him or her to tell you if you start falling behind so that together, you can create a strategy for improvement.

You will be surprised how much better you will start to communicate with the teacher and how much more successful you will be in class.

THINK

If you didn't do well on a test, find a quiet place and think.

Why do you think you didn't do well? Be honest with yourself. Did you study enough? Did you pay attention enough? Did you come to class prepared?

In other words, did you give it 100 percent of your effort?

If you didn't, then resolve to change things. Do you need to study more? Are you spending too much time playing games or socializing?

Change your work ethic towards school.

Take action !

Only you can change your life.

EXERCISE AND NUTRITION

Try and do some form of exercise every day.

Find something you like to do, and you are more likely to do it.

Maybe you play sports. In the off-season, be sure and exercise. It stimulates the mind and keeps our bodies healthy.

If you don't play a sport, find some exercise you like and stick to it.

Be sure and eat healthy every day.

Have breakfast, even if it's only a muffin, a banana, or oatmeal.

Putting food in your body is like putting gas in the car. It works much better with quality fuel.

ON BEING PUNCTUAL

Whether you are ride sharing with a neighbor or friend or getting a ride from your parents, pride yourself on being punctual.

Be completely ready five minutes before the designated time. Have everything you need to take with you waiting at the door. Everybody concerned will be much happier.

Many people don't mind giving rides to others, but it is frustrating to drive to pick them up and then have to wait another ten minutes for them to get ready.

No excuses here. Just be ready early. Plan ahead.

LITTLE THINGS MEAN BIG RESULTS!

How we act leaves an impression on everyone that comes in contact with us. People notice everything we say and how we say it, whether they acknowledge it or register it subconsciously.

You will get much further ahead if you are polite at all times. In fact, it may not seem so at the time, but the more polite you are, the more long-term benefits you will receive.

This not only applies to school but to all aspects of your life, especially your family, friends, classmates, and anyone else that comes in your path.

"Treat others as you would like to be treated" is as vital today as it was hundreds of years ago. Practice it !

AT HOME

It takes so little effort to make a big impression on your parents. Here are some things you can do every day that will really help them out.

Make your bed.
Keep your homework up without being told.
Clean up after yourself.
Take the trash out when it is full.
Keep the bathroom clean.

Ask your parents if there is anything else you can do.

The more successful you are at school, the more privileges you will benefit from.

PLAN OF ACTION
(try it for 30 days)

OK, there is no better time to start raising your grade in school than right now!

Commit yourself to seriously following the guidelines for thirty days. What can you lose? I guarantee that after thirty days, you will be so impressed with yourself, you will have more self-esteem and confidence about school, and this will change your whole outlook on education. You will start enjoying the whole process much more because you will reap the benefits of a good education.

Here's how to start:

School is all about organization.

Start your monthly calendar using your syllabus. If you have lost your syllabus, ask your teacher for a new one.

The more techniques you use from this book, the more successful you will be.

Remember, first impressions are very important.

If you feel you can improve, use today to start making a new first impression.

The night before school, make sure you have the following set out for the next morning in an easy place.

homework
books
pen
notebook
clothes you will wear
jacket (if needed)
lunch
healthy snack
shoes
socks
underwear

Set the alarm for morning. Allow enough time to get up, make your bed, wash, eat breakfast, brush your teeth, and briefly look over your homework for the day.

Go to school with a positive attitude every day and a smile on your face. These will be some of the best memories you will have!

GOING THE EXTRA MILE!

It's important to sit in the front row.

In some classes there is no seating chart, so you must arrive early to get a front-row seat. It is in your best interest not to sit with your friends. You can visit with them at lunch and on breaks, but if you are serious about changing your grade, don't sit with your friends.

If there is a seating chart, you might ask the teacher before class if you can be seated in the front row.

You can also give him or her a note before class. It might read as follows:

Dear Mr. Dominguez,

I want to be successful in your class and earn the best grade possible. May I please be seated in the front row of the classroom so I can focus and listen better?

I promise to be a great student!

Thank you,
Jamel Ortega

JOURNALING
(for students)

Keeping a journal is a very helpful thing for students to do.

Get a notebook, and every night before bed, write in your journal.

Write down all the good things, big and small, that happened that day.

What do you think you did well?

Did you practice a random act of kindness?

Did you learn a new study technique?

Did you improve a friendship?

Start small, and before long you will be writing about more and more good things in your life. Your journal should be just for you—your private thoughts.

Just write good things.

A NEW BEGINNING OF THE REST OF YOUR LIFE

Now that you are practicing all the fantastic principles in this book, you should be much happier both at school and at home.

I can't finish this book without adding the importance of contributing to the world.

Remember, someday you will be ready to pass your wisdom and knowledge to your very own students in your home.

What worked for you? What do you think works best for your family? What would you do differently?

You want to be proud of the world you will put in their hands. In other words, you want to be a good citizen.

Here are some thoughts to think about.

PRACTICE BEING A GOOD CITIZEN, IT'S YOUR WORLD

I am so grateful for all the amazing, wonderful students I have had the opportunity to meet over the years.

They have taught me as much as I have taught them. We have an opportunity to learn wherever we are.

Every student has a story and a lesson we can learn from. Never miss an opportunity to learn from someone that may have a different background or philosophy than you.

Try to leave the world a better place.

If someone filmed you today, would you be proud of your actions? If not, resolve to do better tomorrow.

If each person practiced one new thing a day, the world would change in amazing ways.

PRACTICE GREEN
LIVING

It is amazing how many things I hear in my classes. During breaks and lunch, students talk to each other and offer up lots of information about what is happening in their lives.

One thing that always concerns me and should concern all of us is the way we treat our planet.

It is our responsibility to talk to our students about the importance of conserving our natural resources.

Water:

Research tells us that in the near future, water will be our most valuable resource on the planet, and many of us are not using it wisely.

Many of my students claim to take forty-five minutes or longer in the shower. In their lifetime, they are going to see water become more valuable than oil or any other resource.

Please check and see if you can reduce the time it takes for you and other family members to shower and discuss with them the importance of water co servation and how every person can make a diff ence.

Monitor your sprinklers and check to see that water is not going into the street and that sprinklers are turned off in the rainy season. Every day I see water running in the streets from sprinklers.

Some things we can do right now to conserve water:

When brushing your teeth, turn the water off during those two minutes (the dental association's recommended time for brushing) and then turn it on again when you rinse.

Run your washing machine and dishwasher when full.

Water your lawn in the morning or evening to minimize evaporation. Check your sprinklers to see where the water is going.

Use a timer when watering your lawn.

When you have ice left over in a takeout drink, pour the ice on a plant instead of throwing it in the trash.

Google "water conservation" for more helpful advice.

Ride Sharing:

If you live in a neighborhood with other students going to the same school, meet with the parents and try to devise a ride-sharing plan.

If you do ride share, always be at the door and ready early.

Never make your ride wait; this is very frustrating for the driver and passengers that have a schedule and want to be on time.

Junk Food and Soda:

Most students like to eat junk food and drink soda. Many students eat junk food simply because it's convenient and easy and they don't have healthy choices at home.

If you like soda, try cutting down to one soda a day and replacing the others with water. Your health will benefit from it, and you'll have more energy throughout the day.

Try to always have some healthy food at home to eat and also to take as snacks for school.

Our world is changing so fast.

Our education system is still on what I call "farm time," meaning that one hundred years ago, you went to bed early because there was nothing else to do after dark, then you got up early, did chores, went to school, came home, did chores and homework, and went to bed again. Repeat.

This is how it was, and although so much has changed with modern technology, we have not changed our school time.

We need to realize that students aren't going to bed at dusk anymore, and parents need to speak up at school meetings and address these issues so our students can be more successful.

If I could change one thing about school, I would start school later in the morning and end it later. Extracurricular activities such as sports practice, etc. could be done earlier or later.

Most students stay up late every night. They know who they are, and they know they aren't getting enough sleep, which is why they are always tired in class. (along with poor nutrition and lack of exercise). It is not realistic to think our students are going to bed early. Students are up late on the computer, (whether it is socializing, playing games, having fun, or doing homework), on the phone, or out with friends. Many television shows that students watch are not even on until 10 pm or after.

They may be watching TV, talking on the phone, or all of the above at the same time.

Starting school later would give them time to eat breakfast, review their homework, and arrive at school ready to learn.

FORMS

The following is a list of letters and forms that will be useful in your student's educational process.

Included are samples of letters, thank-you notes, and other communication you may find helpful.

Feel free to copy these directly, substituting your information for what's in the samples.

Or, you may use these as guides to create your own personal notes. Always keep a copy of any communication you send, and be sure and date it.

For more samples please go to the Web site.

www.passtheclass.org

Here are some sample notes on leaving:

Sample 1
DROPPING A CLASS

There are many reasons to quit a class or leave a team or stop going to a study group. Only you can decide if it is the right thing to do, but if you leave with good communication, then when you have that teacher again, he or she will already have a favorable impression of you! Always talk to the teacher or coach in person first if possible.

This is an easy tip that pays off.

Dear Mr. Grimm,

I really enjoyed the brief time I spent in your classroom. I like your teaching style.

Unfortunately, because of scheduling, I have to drop your class.

Thanks for your time and knowledge, and I hope to have the opportunity to take your class again in the future.

Best wishes,

Janet Hernandez

(222) 222-2222

DON'T BURN BRIDGES

If for some reason your student leaves a school activity, always be sure and contact the instructor, coach, team leader, or person in charge.

This is just good manners.

A short phone call or handwritten note is always a good thing to do. You never know when you are going to meet that person again, and you always want to leave a good impression.

Leaving a class or a team, without communicating, or just not showing up anymore, is like burning a bridge.

More than likely, your student will take another class or be on another team or in another study group, and guess who the person in charge will be? Yep, you guessed it. The same teacher or coach.

That's why you always want good honest communication with everyone you associate with.   If you practice this you will always be welcome back on their team or in their class.

Sample 2
LEAVING A SPORTS ACTIVITY

Dear Coach Gomez,

I am glad you understand the reason I have to leave the team.

I think you are a great coach and look forward to having you as a coach in the future!

Best wishes and good luck,

Tim Alexander

Sample 3
SIMPLE THANK-YOU NOTE

Dear Miss Marshall,

Thank you for all the great tutoring you did. I know you put in a lot of effort, and I learned a lot!

All my best wishes, and hope to study with you again soon,

Lila Cruz

MY SCHOOL NETWORK

This is important information that you will need. You will be glad you have a copy of this sheet.

Make a separate page for each student.

Make copies of this page and keep one posted by the phone, in the car, at work, and any other place you may need it.

Student's Name _____

Important Names and Numbers

School _____

School Nurse _____

School Principal _____

Teacher by subject

_____

_____

_____

_____

_____

_____

Doctor _____

Emergency _____

Friends info (name, cell, parents' name, cell)

_____

_____

_____

Please feel free to visit my Web
site and Facebook page:

www.passtheclass.org

**Students under 16 should always be supervised by a
parent when online.**

There are many useful things on the Web site that go
along with this book, including:

blank monthly calendar pages
sample notes for all occasions

forum for sharing your experience and what has
helped you, as well as the chance to learn from others in the same situation, basic and important things
every student should know, including:

how to tie a tie
how to set a dinner table
proper table manners
... and much more.

CONGRATULATIONS!

If you have gotten this far and are practicing the techniques, give yourself an A!

You are better equipped than most of the parents and students at your school.

Keep up the good work and it will become second nature. You and your parents will be very proud of your results and the tremendous change you have made for yourself and the world.

I would love to hear your stories.

Please log in to my Web site and leave your comments in the sharing section.

PASSTHECLASS.ORG

I also invite you to join my *facebook* page .

GLOSSARY

attitude—position of body indicating mental state and feelings, outwardly expressed

body language—nonverbal communicating with others by gestures, poses, and facial expressions

classroom etiquette—acceptable behavior as dictated by the teacher or school

classroom layout—overall design and decor of the room

communicate—transmit thoughts or feelings

effort—conscientious activity intended to accomplish something

extra credit—outside assignment given by teacher to help raise your grade in the class

extracurricular activity—school-related activity usually after school hours (for example, sports, clubs, bands, music, and other social activities)

following up—to follow through on a previous decision or action

goal—intended plan to achieve

journaling—keeping a diary of the day's highlights

modeling—observing a person's behavior

networking—making contacts among friends and other people you know and meet

organize—bring order or structure

participate—be involved and share your ideas and comments

procrastinate—put off until later

rapport—a feeling of being on the same "wavelength" as the person you are talking to

study partner—responsible student in class you can trust to help with assignments and missed work, and that can trust you for same

syllabus—an outline of the course goals and expectations

volunteer—to offer your services or help cheerfully without pay

ABOUT THE AUTHOR

Mr. Grimm has been an educator for thirty years.

He has helped thousands of students
become more successful in school.

He continues to teach in the
western United States.

LaVergne, TN USA
08 February 2011
215733LV00002B/1/P